P9-CQP-306

•*learn it*•
live it
BIBLE STUDIES™

S P I R I T U A L   G I F T S

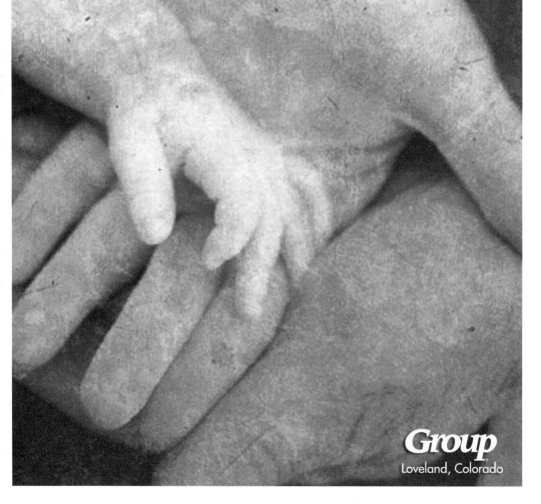

Group
Loveland, Colorado

Group's R.E.A.L. Guarantee® to you:

This Group resource incorporates our R.E.A.L. approach to ministry—one that encourages long-term retention and life transformation. It's ministry that's:

Relational
Because learner-to-learner interaction enhances learning and builds Christian friendships.

Experiential
Because what learners experience through discussion and action sticks with them up to 9 times longer than what they simply hear or read.

Applicable
Because the aim of Christian education is to equip learners to be both hearers and doers of God's Word.

Learner-based
Because learners understand and retain more when the learning process takes into consideration how they learn best.

Learn It, Live It Bible Studies™: Spiritual Gifts
Copyright © 2003 Group Publishing, Inc.

Visit our Web site: **www.grouppublishing.com**

All rights reserved. No part of this book may be reproduced in any manner whatsoever without prior written permission from the publisher, except where noted in the text and in the case of brief quotations embodied in critical articles and reviews. For information, write Permissions, Group Publishing, Inc., Dept. PD, P.O. Box 481, Loveland, CO 80539.

Credits
Contributors: Joe Beckler, Stacey T. Campbell, Ken and Lori Niles, and Paul Woods
Editor: Beth Rowland
Development Editor: Matt Lockhart
Chief Creative Officer: Joani Schultz
Copy Editor: Dena Twinem
Art Director: Randy Kady
Cover Art Director: Jeff A. Storm
Cover Designer: Toolbox Creative
Print Production Artist: Susan Tripp
Cover Photographer: Daniel Treat
Production Manager: Dodie Tipton

Unless otherwise noted, Scripture taken from the HOLY BIBLE, NEW INTERNATIONAL VERSION®. Copyright © 1973, 1978, 1984 by International Bible Society. Used by permission of Zondervan Publishing House. All rights reserved.

ISBN 0-7644-2671-0

10 9 8 7 6 5 4 3 2 1   12 11 10 09 08 07 06 05 04 03

Printed in the United States of America.

Table of Contents

Introduction to Group's
Learn It, Live It Bible Studies™

Welcome to an exciting new concept in small-group Bible studies! At Group, we recognize the value of Bible study to Christian growth—there's no better way to grow in our faith than to study the living Word of God. We also know the value of group activity. Activity helps us practice what we learn. And this is vital to the Christian faith. Jesus doesn't tell us simply to learn about him; he asks us to become like him in thoughts, in words, and in actions. That's why Group developed *Learn It, Live It Bible Studies.* In these studies you'll be challenged to not only learn more about God but also to put what you've learned into practice in a powerful and meaningful way.

Whether you're new to Bible study or a seasoned pro, you'll find the Bible study to be interesting and compelling. In the Bible study section of each lesson, you'll open God's Word with the others in your group. You'll study relevant Scripture passages and discuss thought-provoking questions that will help you all grow in your faith and in your understanding of who God is and what he wants for your life.

After the Bible study, you'll be invited to choose a group project that will help you practice the very thing you've just learned. Some of these projects are simple, easy, and low-risk. Others will require a greater commitment of time and resources; they may take you beyond your comfort zone, too. But whichever group project you choose to do, you can be certain that it will help you grow more like Christ in your everyday life.

We hope you enjoy these lessons! And we pray that by studying these lessons and doing these projects, you'll find yourself becoming more and more like our Lord Jesus Christ.

Spiritual Gifts

This eight-session Bible study focuses on spiritual gifts. The Bible tells us that all who have put their faith in Christ are members of one body. We belong to each other. We are each parts of one unified whole. And just as a body has different parts with different functions, Christians have different roles and gifts. These spiritual gifts come to us from the Holy Spirit through God's grace. Scripture tells us that our gifts are to be used for the common good to build up the body of Christ and prepare it for works of service. Ephesians 4:13 gives us the ultimate goal for the use of spiritual gifts: They are to be used "until we all reach unity in the faith and in the knowledge of the Son of God and become mature, attaining to the whole measure of the fullness of Christ."

Unfortunately, the various interpretations of spiritual gifts seem to cause more division than unity in the church today. Christians hold passionate opinions about spiritual gifts. There are honest differences of opinion about whether the biblical lists are exhaustive, about how the gifts are to be used, and about how many of the biblical gifts are manifested in today's church.

This study seeks to provide an overview of spiritual gifts in a way that will promote unity and discourage needless controversy. While there are three major

Scripture passages that deal with spiritual gifts, this study will focus on Romans 12:3-8. This passage describes seven *serving* or *motivational* gifts. We've chosen this passage as our focus for two primary reasons:

• We want to focus on the practice of these gifts and God's amazing plan for them to be used to build up, unify, and encourage the body.

• The format of these lessons emphasizes giving everyone an opportunity to "try out" each gift and consider whether it's a gift that God has given him or her. The Romans passage lends itself well to this approach.

As a final thought before you dig in to this study, note that Romans 12 begins with this encouragement: "Therefore, I urge you, brothers, in view of God's mercy, to offer your bodies as living sacrifices, holy and pleasing to God—this is your spiritual act of worship." As your group explores the seven spiritual gifts from this passage, let us urge you to make it your goal to wholeheartedly use whatever gifts God has given you as a living, sacrificial act of worship as you serve our gracious, merciful, and loving God!

About the Sessions

Part 1: *learn it*

Start It *(15 minutes)*

This part of the lesson is designed to introduce everyone to the day's topic and to get discussion flowing. Here you'll find an introduction to read and a quick warm-up to do together.

Study It *(45-60 minutes)*

This is the Bible study portion of the lesson. Every lesson provides several Scripture passages to look up and nine to twelve discussion questions for you to talk over as a group. Feel free to jot down your insights in the space provided.

You'll also notice that each lesson includes extra information in the margins. You'll find Bible facts, definitions, and quotations. Please note that the information doesn't always come from a Christian perspective. These margin notes are meant to be thought-provoking and get your group discussing each topic at a deeper level.

Close It *(15-30 minutes)*

During the Close It section of the lesson, you'll do two things. First, you'll read through the Live It options at the end of the lesson and choose one to do together as a group. You'll find more information about the Live It options in the next section.

Second, you'll pray together as a group. Be sure to take the time to listen to one another's prayer requests. You may want to write those prayer requests in the space provided so you can pray for them throughout the week. Don't rush your time with God. Praying with others is a precious opportunity. Make the most of it!

Part 2: live it

In each lesson in this study, you'll find five Live It options. These group activities are designed to help your Bible study group live out what you learned in the Bible study. Together as a group, you'll read over the Live It options each week. Then choose one to do together. You'll find that some of the activities are quick and easy and can be done without planning an extra session. Other activities will require more time and planning. Some activities are very low-risk. Others might push group members to the edge of their comfort zone. Some of the activities are suitable for participation by entire families. Others will work better if you arrange for child care. Choose the option that interests your group the most and carry it out. You'll find that you learn so much more when you practice it in real life.

Spiritual Gifts

There's a lot of confusion in the church today about spiritual gifts. Just the mention of them raises eyebrows among some people but elicits cheers among others. Whatever your perspective on spiritual gifts, it's important that Christians look carefully at what the Bible says about them. Spiritual gifts are given to Christians for the purpose of furthering God's work through the church. If you're sitting in church on the weekend but not using any of your gifts or abilities to serve the God who's reached out to you, then there's something wrong. God intends for each Christian to fully use his or her gifts to further the kingdom and bring glory to God. If you're not using your gifts, you need to consider what gifts God has given you and put them into practice immediately.

On the other hand, if you're at the church numerous times each week to help with many different ministries and activities, perhaps you need to examine where you're *most* gifted and find a way to focus more fully on those areas. God wants each of us to live wholeheartedly for him, but God doesn't intend for any one of us to do it all. This course will help you begin to sort through what spiritual gifts really are. You'll explore the gifts and abilities God has given you, and you'll each help to recognize and confirm the gifts God has given to each member of your group. You'll talk about how God expects Christians to use their gifts, and you'll practice using spiritual gifts through a number of fun projects.

Part 1: *learn it*

Start It *(15 minutes)*
Sweet Gifts

> **Leader:** This is the start of a new study series or perhaps even the beginning of your small group. Take the opportunity to help the members of your group discuss their expectations for the series and the relationships in the group. You might even consider having your group draft a list of expectations for the group, such as attendance and how long you'll meet.

> **Leader:** As people are arriving for your study, have a plate of snacks available for anyone who wants one. Encourage people to help themselves.

To get started on your study, discuss the following questions:

- **How did you like the snacks we started with?**

- **Could you have enjoyed them without taking one, smelling it, and tasting it? Explain.**

- **Do you think we're able to enjoy the spiritual gifts God has given us without using them? Why or why not?**

Study It *(45-60 minutes)*

> If you have a large group, form smaller groups of four to seven people to answer the discussion questions. At the end of the Study It section, allow time for the subgroups to report to the whole group.

1. What do you think of first when someone mentions spiritual gifts? Is that a negative or a positive? Why do you think that is?

Together, quickly read all three of the following passages. Even though it's a lot of reading, it's important to this study.

- *Romans 12:3-13*
- *1 Corinthians 12:1–13:1*
- *Ephesians 4:11-16*

There are three main passages in the New Testament that talk about spiritual gifts. As we do an overview of the topic of spiritual gifts, it's important for everyone to take a look at all three passages to get the broad-stroke look at what the Bible says about them.

2. What do these passages teach about spiritual gifts? What are common themes you read in these passages? What are the differences you see?

3. Why do you think there are differences in the three listings of spiritual gifts? What do you think these differences indicate about the nature of spiritual gifts?

4. In groups of three or four, select one of the passages from page 11, and discuss the following question as related to that passage: If you were a preacher putting together a sermon on spiritual gifts from this passage, what would you say are the three main points you find there? After a few minutes of discussion, tell the whole group what your three points are.

5. What do these main points tell us about spiritual gifts?

Read the statement about spiritual gifts from **The Quest Study Bible.**

6. Do you agree with that statement? Why or why not? How might that thought affect the way you look at your gifts and abilities?

Are spiritual gifts and natural abilities different? "Paul was probably unconcerned about distinguishing between physical and spiritual abilities. To him all gifts, 'natural' or 'supernatural,' came from God. The central issue for Paul was people using their abilities to build up and strengthen the church."

The Quest Study Bible

7. How does the overarching principle of love, mentioned in all three of the passages we've looked at today, affect the way we look at and use spiritual gifts in the church?

8. After all we've seen on spiritual gifts in this quick overview, what has been the biggest surprise? How will that change the way you look at spiritual gifts?

Close It *(15-30 minutes)*

Review the options in the Live It section of this session, and make plans as a group to complete one of these activities prior to moving on to the next session. This is your opportunity to move from theory to practice—*carpe diem!*

Pray It

Share prayer requests, and close in prayer. Be sure to ask God to guide your efforts as you plan and carry out a Live It activity.

Plan It

What activity are we going to do?

When are we doing this?

Where will this take place?

Other: special instructions/my responsibility

Option 1

Plan a time together during which you will play an active team game, such as softball, volleyball, touch football, basketball, or soccer. If your group isn't physically capable of playing such games, consider playing a team game such as Pictionary, Cranium, or Guesstures. Afterward, talk about the importance of each player on the team. Compare the team-nature of the sport or game to the team-nature of using spiritual gifts in the church.

Option 2

Have each person study the Bible passages in this lesson and pray through the week about what spiritual gifts he or she might have. When you gather again, have each person bring an item representing what he or she feels one of his or her spiritual gifts might be, as well as a plan for using that spiritual gift. Spend your time having each person report and having others share their ideas for how that person might be able to use his or her gifts in ministry or service to others.

Option 3

Have your pastor or another church leader come to your next session to discuss ministry needs in the church and the types of gifts needed to run or participate in those ministries. Spend your time talking through your group's spiritual gifts and how they might match up with your church's ministry needs. Be sure to spend plenty of time in prayer, asking God to guide each of you in putting your gifts into practice.

Option 4

Do a spiritual gifts inventory. Several different kinds are available, either at your local Christian bookstore or on the Internet. You may want to consult your church or pastor for a recommendation. Have each person go through the inventory to help determine what spiritual gifts he or she has. Then discuss your test results. Talk about how each person might be able to better use his or her spiritual gifts within your church.

Option 5

Plan a service project in which the group has an opportunity to experience a variety of gifts. For example, you might go to a homeless shelter for an evening. Some would be able to serve meals, others might organize activities for children, some might give a talk or a message, some others might present a concert of praise music, and still others might sit down and talk one-on-one with some of the people gathered there.

Afterward, talk about the gifts you saw in action and what you observed about how God used the people in the group.

Debrief It

After experiencing this session's Live It activity, discuss these questions as a group:

- **On a scale of 1 (low) to 10 (high), how would you rank this experience for yourself? Why?**

- **What was the most important insight you gained from this experience?**

- **How did our activity affect the way you think about your own spiritual gifts?**

- **How might this activity change your involvement in ministry?**

Journal It

The following space is provided for you to record your personal thoughts, reflections, impressions, or feelings about this session's topic and Live It activity.

Prophecy

The gift of prophecy is largely misunderstood by people in the church today. Some feel it only refers to the future predictions of Old Testament prophets, but that is clearly false. While there are many misconceptions about prophecy, there are also differences of opinion about prophecy that all fall within an orthodox interpretation of Scripture.

Some Christians believe that God still reveals the future to some people today. The prophet Agabus predicted future happenings at least twice (Acts 11:27-28; 21:10-11). God revealed the future to Paul at least twice (Acts 18:9-11; 27:14-44). And God gave to John the book of Revelation, which is filled with predictive prophecy.

Other Christians believe that gifts such as miracles, healing, tongues, and predictive prophecy ceased either at the end of the time when the apostles lived (2 Corinthians 12:12) or when Scripture was complete (1 Corinthians 13:8-10).

The word *prophecy* does not only refer to telling the future. It can also be inspired speech that strengthens, encourages, and comforts (1 Corinthians 14:3). The Greek word used in Romans 12:6 indicates that prophecy is the "speaking forth of the mind and counsel of God."

This lesson will focus on the non-predictive meanings of the word *prophecy* so that everyone in your group can practice this gift. In this session, we'll seek to clear up some of the misconceptions people have about prophecy, and we'll explore what it means to have the gift of prophecy today.

Start It *(15 minutes)*

Profound Insights

Begin your study by telling stories. Share a story about a time you had a profound insight into Scripture or a time someone else had a profound insight into Scripture that was inspirational or meaningful to you.

Then discuss the following questions:

- **How did either prophesying yourself or hearing prophecy from someone else affect your life and your relationship with God?**

- **What makes a statement prophetic?**

- **Have you ever felt that you have the gift of prophecy? Why or why not?**

> "Though much of O.T. (Old Testament) prophecy was purely predictive... prophecy is not necessarily, nor even primarily, fore-telling. It is the declaration of that which cannot be known by natural means, Matt. 26:68, it is the forth-telling of the will of God, whether with reference to the past, the present, or the future."
>
> *Vine's Expository Dictionary of Old and New Testament Words*

Study It *(45-60 minutes)*

> If you have a large group, form smaller groups of four to seven people to answer the discussion questions. At the end of the Study It section, allow time for the subgroups to report to the whole group.

Read Romans 12:6 and the margin note.

1. What is prophecy? Does the definition in the margin change the way you look at prophecy?

2. Do you believe God ever gives people the power to see into the future today? Why or why not?

3. Who would you consider to be prophets in the church today? Explain.

4. Form pairs or trios, and divide the following list of verses among you. Read your verses and note what you learn about prophecy. After a few minutes, summarize your verses and share your ideas with the rest of the group.

   • *Acts 2:17-21*
   • *Acts 13:1-5*
   • *1 Corinthians 14:1-5*
   • *1 Corinthians 14:22-25*

> "The words the prophet utters are not offered as souvenirs...In speaking, the prophet reveals God. This is the marvel of a prophet's work: in his words, *the invisible God becomes audible...*Divine power bursts in the words. The authority of the prophet is in the Presence his words reveal."
>
> **Abraham J. Heschel, *The Prophets***

Read the quote from **The Prophets.**

5. Heschel wrote this book referring primarily to Old Testament prophets. What does it say about the importance of prophecy? How does this quote apply to people with the gift of prophecy today?

6. Read 1 Corinthians 13:2. What perspective does this verse add to the place of prophecy and how it should be used?

Read the following verses:
- *Acts 2:17*
- *Acts 13:1*
- *Acts 21:8-9*

7. Who can prophesy? What might be some limits on who can prophesy?

8. What is the primary role of someone with the gift of prophecy today? What opportunities for using that gift are available in the church today?

9. How effectively is the gift of prophecy being used in the church today?

10. What should a person who believes he or she has the gift of prophecy do to develop and use this gift?

Close It *(15-30 minutes)*

Review the options in the Live It section of this session, and make plans as a group to complete one of these activities prior to moving on to the next session. This is your opportunity to move from theory to practice—*carpe diem!*

Pray It

Share prayer requests, and close in prayer. Be sure to ask God to guide your efforts as you plan and carry out a Live It activity.

Plan It

What activity are we going to do?

When are we doing this?

Where will this take place?

Other: special instructions/my responsibility

Part 2: live it

Option 1

Make plans to gather one evening. Have each person bring a book or tape or writing he or she feels is prophetic. Have each person explain why he or she feels the item is prophetic and how it has affected his or her life. Then have the group evaluate it. Do you all agree about the items? Why or why not? Discuss whether one piece of prophecy should apply to all Christians.

Option 2

Allow everyone to practice prophecy. Have each person choose a passage of Scripture to read and pray over through the week and then prepare a three- to five-minute message based on what God has revealed to him or her from that passage. At your next session, encourage each other to present the messages. Be kind to every-one who presents, and applaud each person for having the courage to get up in front of the group. If the message really speaks to you, let the person and the group know. Then discuss how to know whether you or someone else has the gift of prophecy.

Option 3

This activity is based on the definition of prophecy from the introduction (prophecy is the speaking forth of the mind and counsel of God). Plan for a time when everyone can gather for about an hour. Have each person spend time praying and search-ing the Scripture for the answers to these questions:
- What does God think about the direction our church is going?
- What does God think about the status of our society and our country?
- What does God think about the international situation today?

After fifteen or twenty minutes of reflection, discuss each ques-tion with the entire group. Did anyone have a particularly insight-ful comment? Did you all agree about God's opinion? Do your thoughts agree with Scripture? How does this discussion apply to the idea of prophecy?

Option 4

Identify a person in your church or community you all feel has the gift of prophecy. Invite that person to come to your group to discuss the spiritual gift of prophecy. Ask your guest, "How do you know you have the gift of prophecy, and how have you been able to use that gift to serve the church?" Then ask your guest to share with you any insights he or she has about your study, about Scripture in general, or about God. Be sure to evaluate anything your guest says with Scripture.

Option 5

For those in the group who believe they might have the gift of prophecy, arrange a discussion with your church's leadership. Encourage all involved to give these people a chance to begin exercising the gift in appropriate ways. If further training would be helpful, encourage them to pursue it, and see if your church is able to give any kind of assistance with the training.

Debrief It

After experiencing this session's Live It activity, discuss these questions as a group:

- **On a scale of 1 (low) to 10 (high), how would you rank this experience for yourself? Why?**

- **What was the most important insight you gained from this experience?**

- **How did our activity affect the way you think about your own spiritual gifts?**

- **How might this activity change your involvement in ministry?**

- **Who in this group do you feel has the gift of prophecy? Explain.**

Journal It

The following space is provided for you to record your personal thoughts, reflections, impressions, or feelings about this session's topic and Live It activity.

Serving

Our society today isn't much into serving. Even when we think that we are servant-hearted people, we are often more genuinely concerned about ourselves than we are about others. But that's not God's way. When Jesus lived on earth, he served people by healing those who others wouldn't even come near. He taught and healed patiently though he was often pushed to the point of exhaustion. He washed his disciples' feet—the job of a servant. He ultimately served people by giving up his own life on the cross so that those who believe in him can have eternal life.

The Bible tells us that Jesus is the ultimate example of how Christians are to live. We are to become as Christlike as possible while we live here on earth. But imitating perfection is a tough job! Nevertheless, we are called to love and serve as Christ did. And that especially holds true for those who have the spiritual gift of service. Though we all have the responsibility to serve God and others, some people have a special gift for serving. In this session, we'll take a look at what it means to have that gift, and we'll seek to evaluate what sets apart someone with that gift from all the other Christians serving God.

Part 1: learn it

Start It *(15 minutes)*

It's Your Serve

> **Leader:** For this session, arrange for some sort of snack that must be eaten with a fork or a spoon.

To start today's session, find a partner. Bring a snack to your partner and feed it to him or her bite by bite. Then let your partner serve you.

After you're finished with the snack, discuss these questions:

- • What did you think about serving a snack to your partner? about being served?

- • What's difficult about serving someone else?

- • What's good about serving someone else?

Study It *(45-60 minutes)*

> If you have a large group, form smaller groups of four to seven people to answer the discussion questions. At the end of the Study It section, allow time for the subgroups to report to the whole group.

Read Romans 12:1-7.

1. What does serving have to do with the body of Christ?

2. What would you say are the main characteristics of someone who has the gift of serving?

3. Form pairs or trios, and divide the following list of verses among you. Read your verses and note what you learn about serving. Also discuss whether those principles apply to all Christians or only to those with the gift of serving. After a few minutes, summarize your verses and share your ideas with the rest of the group.

- *Acts 6:1-7*
- *Galatians 5:13-14*
- *Philippians 2:3-4*
- *1 Peter 4:10-11*

The Greek word translated "serving" in Romans 12:7 indicates someone who serves, particularly by carrying out the commands of others. This is not the word for a slave, but instead it indicates a voluntary serving, sometimes particularly related to serving God.

Read the margin note about serving.

4. What light does this explanation shed on the topic of serving?

5. In your pairs or trios, divide the following list of verses among you. Read your verses and note what you learn about serving. After a few minutes, summarize your verses and share your ideas with the rest of the group.

- *Luke 23:50-54*
- *John 13:1-5*
- *Acts 9:36-39*
- *2 Timothy 1:16-18*

Read the margin note.

6. How is the gift of service different from everyone's responsibility to serve God?

7. What types of roles in your church (or in your small group) do you believe are filled by people with the gift of serving?

All of us are responsible to serve one another, no matter what gifts we have. In fact, serving one another is a principle for using any spiritual gift. However, someone with the gift of serving is likely someone who enjoys staying in the background, working in what might be considered menial chores, without worrying about rewards or praise. This person probably prefers staying out of the limelight and serving faithfully and quietly.

8. If you had the gift of serving, what opportunities for service would there be for you in the church? in your community? in the world?

9. What impact do you see the gift of serving having on our church? our community? the world?

Close It *(15-30 minutes)*

Review the options in the Live It section of this session, and make plans as a group to complete one of these activities prior to moving on to the next session. This is your opportunity to move from theory to practice—*carpe diem!*

Pray It

Share prayer requests, and close in prayer. Be sure to ask God to guide your efforts as you plan and carry out a Live It activity.

Plan It

What activity are we going to do?

When are we doing this?

Where will this take place?

Other: special instructions/my responsibility

Option 1

Spend time serving one another. Have each person come to your next session with something he or she can do to serve the rest of your group. That might be bringing a plate of cookies, giving people shoulder rubs, or serving drinks. Consider having one person coordinate everyone's efforts so that not everyone brings a snack. Talk about how it feels to serve others and to be served. Also talk about the different ways the gift of service manifests itself in the body of Christ.

Option 2

Plan a time to serve your church. For example, you might serve doughnuts and coffee or sandwiches and soft drinks to the entire congregation after a worship service. You might do the weekly cleaning of the building. You might wash the windshields of every car in the parking lot.

Option 3

Discover people who have the gift of serving and are already quietly serving behind the scenes at your church. Plan a way to honor them with a special gift of service. For example, you might rake their lawns or provide a special meal. You might provide before-church child care for those who work during the church service and come early to prepare. You might take over their responsibilities at the church for a week.

Option 4

Put each group member's name in a hat. Draw names. Have each person in the group do an act of service for the person whose name he or she drew. To do this, have each person talk with the person whose name they drew during the week to find out what kind of service would be appreciated. For example, a busy parent might appreciate having someone cook dinner and clean the kitchen one night. Someone who has to travel for business this week might appreciate having someone pick up the mail or mow the yard. Someone who's new to the area might appreciate an afternoon spent exploring the town and being shown the best restaurants, shops, and recreational activities. Do your best to tailor these acts of service for each person's particular situation.

Option 5

Before your session, have someone gather from your church leaders a list of serving roles that need to be filled in your church. At your meeting, explore what each of those roles entails, and offer opportunities for those having the gift of serving. Be sure the group doesn't lay guilt on those who don't respond to the opportunities. Not everyone has the gift of service, and some may be serving in many ways already.

Debrief It

After experiencing this session's Live It activity, discuss these questions as a group:

- **On a scale of 1 (low) to 10 (high), how would you rank this experience for yourself? Why?**

- **What was the most important insight you gained from this experience?**

- **How did our activity affect the way you think about your own spiritual gifts?**

- **How might this activity change your involvement in ministry?**

- **Who in this group do you think has the gift of serving? Explain.**

Journal It

The following space is provided for you to record your personal thoughts, reflections, impressions, or feelings about this session's topic and Live It activity.

Teaching

The final earthly command of Jesus has to do not only with making disciples, but also with teaching them (Matthew 28:19-20). Teaching is central to the mission of the church. But the questions "What can we know?" and "How do we come to know?" are central to four spiritual gifts: teaching, wisdom, knowledge, and discernment. Often these gifts that deal with the branch of philosophical thought known as *epistemology* are addressed together, since one who teaches must possess some degree of content knowledge, the wisdom to know how to apply that knowledge to life experience, and discernment to understand the mind of Christ in relation to the spirits of humanity. It is possible for a believer to have the gifts of wisdom, knowledge, or discernment without having the gift of teaching, but this cluster of gifts often comes together in service to the body of Christ.

Teaching in the church happens in many ways. It happens as the older believer mentors the younger. It happens as a teacher meets in a weekly session with a group of believers in a classroom setting. It happens informally as believers share their faith over coffee. It happens as pastors proclaim truth from the pulpit. It happens in the formal educational settings of school and university. No matter the setting, the goal of Christian teaching is the development of maturity in the mental, spiritual, emotional, and behavioral life of the believer. Teaching changes lives.

This lesson will give you the opportunity to explore some of the many different facets of teaching and to appreciate God's plan for keeping the message of the good news alive through the generations.

Start It *(15 minutes)*

If You Can Read This, Thank a Teacher

> **Leader:** Before class, gather a selection of stationery or thank-you notes, envelopes, stamps, and pens.

Take one of the thank-you notes your leader has provided, and write a brief expression of appreciation to someone who taught you something that has proven to be valuable in your life. After about five minutes, share who you chose to write to and why you chose to write to that teacher. After today's study, take time to locate the person you wrote to, and mail the thank-you note as an affirmation of that individual's influence in your life.

Next, discuss these questions:

- **Why do we have such passionate feelings, whether positive or negative, about the teachers we've had?**

- **When have you found yourself in the role of teacher? Was the experience positive or negative? Explain.**

- **Which do you enjoy more, being the learner or the teacher? Why?**

Study It *(45-60 minutes)*

> If you have a large group, form smaller groups of four to seven people to answer the discussion questions. At the end of the Study It section, allow time for the subgroups to report to the whole group.

Read the margin note. Also read
Ecclesiastes 7:12 and Philippians 1:9-11.

1. Why are learning, knowledge, and wisdom so important to God?

There are at least twenty-four different original-language words in the Bible that pertain to teaching, learning, and knowing. Each of these words reveals a nuance of the process. Some of these words are roughly translated as proclaiming, directing, warning, applying, actively involving, mind-shaping, edifying, expounding, interpreting, opening, guiding, cleaving, and understanding.

Read Romans 12:3-8.

2. What role does the spiritual gift of teaching have in the body of Christ?

3. Form pairs or trios, and divide the following list of verses among you. Read your verses and note what you learn about teaching. After a few minutes, summarize your verses and share your ideas with the rest of the group.

  • *Exodus 35:30-35*
  • *Ecclesiastes 12:9-11*
  • *Romans 2:17-23*
  • *Colossians 3:16-17*
  • *2 Timothy 2:2*

Read John 13:1-5, 12-17.

4. Why is it significant that Jesus identified himself as a teacher? What can you learn from Jesus' example as a teacher?

Read the margin note.

5. What do good teachers do? What traits do they have? Be as complete as you can with your answer.

"I had forgotten that what people need is not unlimited access to information; they need interpretation. One can reach a point where he has so much information that he doesn't know anything at all."

Erwin R. McManus, *An Unstoppable Force*

Read Romans 15:14.

6. What can a good teacher accomplish?

7. What are the differences between good and bad teachers?

Read the margin note.

8. Form pairs or trios, and divide the following list of verses among you. Read your verses and note what cautions or responsibilities for teachers you find. After a few minutes, summarize your verses and share your ideas with the rest of the group.

- *Isaiah 29:13*
- *Luke 6:39-40*
- *Acts 15:1*
- *Acts 18:25*

- *I Timothy 6:3-5*
- *Titus 1:9*
- *James 3:1-2*

"Reduce teaching to intellect, and it becomes a cold abstraction; reduce it to emotions, and it becomes narcissistic; reduce it to the spiritual, and it loses its anchor to the world. Intellect, emotion, and spirit depend on one another for wholeness."

Parker J. Palmer, *The Courage to Teach*

9. Other than teachers, who might have the spiritual gift of teaching?

10. Have you ever felt that you have the spiritual gift of teaching? Why or why not? What should a person with the gift of teaching do to practice and develop it?

Close It *(15-30 minutes)*

Review the options in the Live It section of this session, and make plans as a group to complete one of these activities prior to moving on to the next session. This is your opportunity to move from theory to practice—*carpe diem!*

Pray It

Share prayer requests, and close in prayer. Be sure to ask God to guide your efforts as you plan and carry out a Live It activity.

Plan It

What activity are we going to do?

When are we doing this?

Where will this take place?

Other: special instructions/my responsibility

Option 1

The teaching spoken of in Exodus 35:34 relates to a particular set of craft-based skills that were relevant to the creation of the house of God.

Determine what craft-based skills are represented in your group, and offer to host a one-day teaching workshop for your congregation (or for each other) in which members of your group will share a craft with those who are interested in learning.

Option 2

Individually or in groups of two or three, make arrangements to shadow a teacher for an afternoon or even a full day. You may want to shadow your child's teacher, a teacher you know from the congregation, or a university professor whose specialty is of particular interest to you. Pay attention to how the teacher presents material and interacts with students. Talk to the teacher about what he or she finds rewarding and challenging about teaching. Consider what tips you can pick up to use in the situations where you find yourself teaching others.

Option 3

Teachers in public schools are usually required to keep up their skills by attending professional-development classes. Find out what classes your church and your local colleges and universities offer for developing teaching skills. Sign up for a class, and develop your skills. If there are no classes being held right away, you may want to visit your local library and check out a book on effective teaching methods.

Option 4

Adopt your local church library. Assess the resources offered in your library. Are they current? attractively arranged? accessible to a cross section of your congregation? If you find that your resources are lacking, sponsor a library renovation "shower" through which the congregation is encouraged to donate resources and materials for effective research and study. You may want to suggest that your church promote its resources by putting book reviews in the weekly bulletin or newsletter. Educate your congregation by having each member of your group choose a book from the library and write a review.

Option 5

Offer yourselves as teacher assistants in the children's and youth departments for a week, month, or quarter. Be prepared to assist in any way the teacher asks, from interacting with a specific child to helping with classroom decoration, or substitute teaching for a session. You may find that you love teaching. If you don't enjoy the experience, try again with another age level.

Debrief It

After experiencing this session's Live It activity, discuss these questions as a group:

- **On a scale of 1 (low) to 10 (high), how would you rank this experience for yourself? Why?**

- **What was the most important insight you gained from this experience?**

- **How did our activity affect the way you think about your own spiritual gifts?**

- **How might this activity change your involvement in ministry?**

- **Who in this group may have the gift of teaching? Explain.**

Journal It

The following space is provided for you to record your personal thoughts, reflections, impressions, or feelings about this session's topic and Live It activity.

Encouragement

We do not live in an encouraging world. It's probably more apt to describe our environment as a rat race rather than as a society of encouragement and nurture. It's not that we don't value encouragement or understand its power. It's that our society works on a system of competitiveness. Too often in our world, it seems people get ahead by trouncing their peers. As if that weren't enough to discourage us, take into consideration that we also must battle against the forces of nature, the forces of bureaucracy, and the forces of evil. Life is definitely an uphill battle.

Those who exercise the spiritual gift of encouragement are like cool water to the parched and weary soul. Encouragement can empower the defeated to victory and give those who suffer a reason to live. Encouragers possess a spiritual power to release the light of God's hope in a world of darkness.

In this lesson, you'll look at the spiritual gift of encouragement and see what the Bible has to say about this powerful gift. Through the Live It opportunities, you'll also experience firsthand how the life-giving power of encouragement can revolutionize our lives as well as the world around us.

Start It *(15 minutes)*

Powerful Words

Begin today's session with this brainstorming activity. Have someone keep time for three minutes while the group goes around the circle and brainstorms words of *discouragement*. Then have someone keep time for another three minutes while the group goes around the circle the other way and brainstorms words of *encouragement*.

Then discuss these questions:

- **Was it easier to think of encouraging words or discouraging words? Explain.**

- **When have you felt utterly discouraged? How did that affect your life?**

- **When have you felt truly encouraged? How did that affect your life?**

> Romans 12:8 uses the Greek word *paraklesis* to describe the spiritual gift of encouragement, which is also commonly referred to as the gift of exhortation. This word carries a multifaceted meaning, including the following:
>
> - to call on, entreat
> - to admonish
> - to urge one to pursue some course of conduct
> - to comfort

Study It *(45-60 minutes)*

> If you have a large group, form smaller groups of four to seven people to answer the discussion questions. At the end of the Study It section, allow time for the subgroups to report to the whole group.

Read the margin note.

1. Describe what encouragement is and isn't, putting it in real-life terms.

2. Who do you know who is an encourager? How does he or she encourage? What can you learn from this person's example?

Read Romans 12:3-8.

3. What role does the gift of encouragement have in the body of Christ?

Read Colossians 4:7-8 and I Thessalonians 3:2.

4. Consider the environment of the early church and the mode of travel. Why was encouragement such a priority? Do we give encouragement the same importance in our churches today? Why or why not?

5. Why is encouragement necessary? What does encouragement accomplish?

learn it
live it

Read Acts 4:36-37; Acts 9:26-27; and Acts 11:19-26.

6. How did Barnabas prove himself to be an encourager? What can you learn from his example?

"The connectedness of a community is such that the devaluation and dehumanization of one is the devaluation and dehumanization of all."

Leonard Sweet,
AquaChurch

Read the margin note.

7. Do you agree that the way one person is treated has an effect on the larger community? Explain.

8. Encouragement is a recurring topic in the book of 1 Thessalonians. Form pairs or trios, and divide the following list of verses among you. Read your verses and note why the Thessalonian Christians needed encouragement, how Paul encouraged them, and the reasons Paul encouraged them to encourage each other. After a few minutes, summarize your verses and share your ideas with the rest of the group.

- *1 Thessalonians 2:17–3:3*
- *1 Thessalonians 4:13-18*
- *1 Thessalonians 5:4-11*
- *1 Thessalonians 5:12-24*

9. Divide the following passages among the same subgroups. Read your verses and note what you learn about how to encourage others. After a few minutes, summarize your verses and share your ideas with the rest of the group.

- *2 Timothy 4:1-5*
- *Titus 1:7-9*
- *Titus 2:6-8, 15*
- *Hebrews 3:12-13*
- *Hebrews 10:23-25*

10. Have you ever felt that you have the gift of encouragement? Why or why not?

11. What should a person with the gift of encouragement do to practice and develop this gift?

Close It *(15-30 minutes)*

Review the options in the Live It section of this session, and make plans as a group to complete one of these activities prior to moving on to the next session. This is your opportunity to move from theory to practice—*carpe diem!*

Pray It

Share prayer requests, and close in prayer. Be sure to ask God to guide your efforts as you plan and carry out a Live It activity.

Plan It

What activity are we going to do?

When are we doing this?

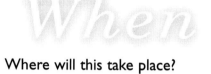

Where will this take place?

Other: special instructions/my responsibility

Option 1

As a group, take turns showering each other with words of encouragement. Sit in a circle. Select someone as the "person to be encouraged." Have group members each say something encouraging to the person. The person being encouraged is not allowed to speak or respond to any comments made. He or she must simply listen and receive the comments. After everyone has had an opportunity to share, select another person to be encouraged. Repeat this process for everyone in the group.

Option 2

Spend a few minutes discussing practical ways to show encouragement to others. Then have each person in the group choose at least one person to purposefully encourage throughout this week. It may be a parent, spouse, child, friend, or co-worker. You may want to choose several people to encourage. For example, you might choose to encourage someone who lacks confidence, someone who's very dear to you, and someone you dislike. Do or say at least one encouraging thing to each person you choose every day of the week. At the end of the week, evaluate the experience. Did the person benefit from or appreciate your encouragement? How did your encouragement affect your attitude toward the person? Would you like to continue encouraging that person? Should you broaden your circle of encouragement?

Option 3

As a group, pick a group of people who work in thankless jobs and are not often appreciated. Plan a celebration for them. For example, you might want to thank the paramedics who work in your area. You may want to thank the custodial staff or the nursery workers at your church or the teachers at a local high school or the staff at a homeless shelter. Another idea would be to recognize those in your church who have one of the other spiritual gifts. For example, you might want to encourage your church's leaders and teachers.

For the celebration, consider sending a "party in a box." Choose a very large box. In the bottom, place party food such as a cake or cookies, chips, soda pop in tightly closed bottles, and paper goods. Put in a CD of fun party music. Next have each member of your group put in a card with an encouraging note. Fill the box to the top with inflated balloons, confetti, and party streamers. Seal the box, put a note on the top explaining what's inside, and have everyone use markers to decorate the outside of the box. Then deliver the box, and have a party.

Option 4

Encouragement ultimately has to do with challenging people to a deeper walk with God. Think and pray about the people God has placed in your life. Identify one person with whom you could work to develop a close encouraging relationship. Determine where this person is in his or her faith journey. Is this person skeptical, investigating the faith, a new believer, reconnecting with the church, or a seasoned veteran of the faith?

Invite that person out for coffee or a soft drink, and talk about whether the person would be willing to enter into such a relationship with you. You may want to propose that you meet together weekly for a period of four to six weeks to simply talk about your relationships with God.

Keep in mind the following:

• Be a good friend. Establish a foundation of love and care before ever expecting an opportunity to talk about spiritual things.

• Remember to value the person more than the opportunity to practice being an encourager.

• Have realistic expectations. Don't expect this person to be like you or to have the same passion for God that you do. And don't seek to change him or her or be dictating. Your role is to be a loving encourager.

• Be a good listener. Show you care by taking interest.

• Package your encouragement in such a way that this person can easily understand spiritual concepts. Don't go over his or her head. Don't condescend, either.

• Keep the meetings casual. Between meetings touch base with the person you are discipling. Use notes, phone calls, and e-mail.

• Don't forget to pray about this relationship and what God wants you to say and do.

Option 5

An often-forgotten part of the spiritual gift of encouragement is the responsibility to correct others in love. The encourager is one who challenges others forward in their faith. Forward spiritual growth sometimes requires a gentle push from a caring encourager.

Form pairs. Your partner will be your accountability partner. Talk through the confrontational side of encouragement. Share where you need to be pushed in order to grow in your spiritual walk. Agree to gently and respectfully push each other in your spiritual walk this week.

Touch base with your partner at least three times during the week. Respectfully "speak the truth in love" to your partner and encourage him or her to do whatever needs to be done to grow spiritually.

Debrief It

After experiencing this session's Live It activity, discuss these questions as a group:

- **On a scale of 1 (low) to 10 (high), how would you rank this experience for yourself? Why?**

- **What was the most important insight you gained from this experience?**

- **How did our activity affect the way you think about your own spiritual gifts?**

- **How might this activity change your involvement in ministry?**

- **Who in this group do you think has the gift of encouragement? Explain.**

The following space is provided for you to record your personal thoughts, reflections, impressions, or feelings about this session's topic and Live It activity.

Contributing to the Needs of Others

People respond to the concept of giving to others with very strong emotions. On occasion we are so moved with love and compassion for others that we give generously and sacrificially. However, it may be more common that we feel a defensive recoil within our spirit at the thought of letting go of our possessions. We tend to hold on to them very tightly. Our tendency toward possessiveness affects our spirituality. Jesus clearly communicates in his ministry that money and possessions are often where the tug-of-war battle for the soul is fought (Matthew 19:16-24).

All Christians are called to give cheerfully and generously. But in Romans 12:8, the Apostle Paul mentions contributing to others' needs as one of the gifts of the Holy Spirit. Apparently some Christians have a special ability to both understand what others need and to use the resources God has given them to meet those needs. Those who have the spiritual gift of giving to others often experience special joy in meeting others' needs.

There is much advice in Scripture about how we are to treat our money and our possessions and the generous nature we are to cultivate. God is pleased when we share what we have with others. In this lesson, you'll explore what the Bible has to say about this spiritual gift. Then you'll practice contributing to the needs of others and explore whether you might be blessed with this gift.

Start It *(15 minutes)*

Give It Away?

Search your pockets, your wallet, or your purse to determine how much money you have access to at this moment. Don't forget to include the credit limits of any credit cards you have with you and the balance in your checking account if you have your checkbook with you. You don't need to tell the group the figure you come up with, just have that amount in mind for the following discussion.

Discuss these questions with the rest of the group.

- **What kind of need or crisis would prompt you to generously tap into the money you have available to you at this moment?**

- **Consider the money you give to meet others' needs. Do you consider yourself to be a generous and compassionate giver? Why or why not?**

- **Describe the most generous person you know. Do you think that person is wise in the way he or she handles money? Explain.**

Study It *(45-60 minutes)*

> If you have a large group, form smaller groups of four to seven people to answer the discussion questions. At the end of the Study It section, allow time for the subgroups to report to the whole group.

Read Romans 12:3-8.

1. How would you define and describe the gift of contributing to the needs of others?

2. What role does the spiritual gift of giving to others play in the body of Christ?

3. Do you know anyone you think has this gift? What does this person do that indicates he or she has the gift of contributing to the needs of others?

4. What's the difference between the giving that all Christians are to do and the spiritual gift of giving that only some are blessed with?

Compare Acts 2:42-47 and Acts 4:32-35 with Mark 10:17-25.

5. What can happen when we give generously? What can happen when we don't?

6. Form pairs or trios, and divide the following list of verses among you. Read your verses and note what you learn about generously contributing to the needs of others. After a few minutes, summarize your verses and share your ideas with the rest of the group.

- *2 Corinthians 8:1-5*
- *2 Corinthians 8:6-9*
- *2 Corinthians 8:10-15*
- *2 Corinthians 9:6-11*
- *2 Corinthians 9:12-15*

Read the margin note and Isaiah 58:6-12.

7. Describe all that it means to contribute to the needs of others.

> The phrase "give generously" in Romans 12:8 is best understood as dealing with one's attitude. Paul is suggesting that the one who gives should do so with pure motives, no agenda, and a glad heart.

8. What are the spiritual and practical results when we contribute generously to the needs of others?

Read Luke 12:27-34.

9. What can hinder us from giving to others? How can we set aside those hindrances and give generously? What happens when we do?

10. Have you ever felt that you have this spiritual gift? Explain. How might one with this spiritual gift practice and develop it?

Close It *(15-30 minutes)*

Review the options in the Live It section of this session, and make plans as a group to complete one of these activities prior to moving on to the next session. This is your opportunity to move from theory to practice—*carpe diem!*

Pray It

Share prayer requests, and close in prayer. Be sure to ask God to guide your efforts as you plan and carry out a Live It activity.

Plan It

What activity are we going to do?

When are we doing this?

Where will this take place?

Other: special instructions/my responsibility

Option 1

Each person or couple should spend time reviewing how they plan to spend their income for this month. Each person or couple should also spend time investigating who in the church or community might have a financial need. Everyone is then encouraged to take money that's already earmarked for a nonessential purchase (for example, a vacation, videos, CDs, or clothes) and give it away to someone who has need of the money. No one needs to tell how much money he or she gave away, but everyone should report what he or she had planned to put the money toward, who he or she gave the money to, and what happened as a result of contributing to someone else's need.

Option 2

Follow this schedule of giving to others:

Day One: Find one item in your home, and give it to someone who could better use it. Make sure you give away a useful, unbroken item. Do not replace the item you give away.

Day Two: Find two items in your home, and give them away.

Day Three: Find three items, and give them away.

Day Four: Find four items, and give them away.

Day Five: Find five items, and give them away.

Day Six: Find six items, and give them away.

Day Seven: Find seven items, and give them away.

By the end of the week, you'll have given away twenty-eight items. A couple who does this activity separately will have given away fifty-six items. A group of ten people doing this activity will give away 280 items!

At the end of the week, gather to discuss this activity. Was it easy or difficult to find this many things to part with? Did it get harder or easier through the week? How do you feel now about how much stuff you have? Is this a discipline you could incorporate in your life regularly?

Option 3

Giving to others can be very rewarding. But it's too easy for the giver to be completely removed from the recipient. Giving to others face to face brings extra challenges and extra rewards. Pray and talk together about where your group can spend time giving to others. You may agree to spend an evening talking with the elderly at a nursing home or with patients at a VA hospital. You may spend an afternoon working at an inner-city after-school club or you may choose to adopt a refugee family and help them acclimate to life in this country.

Option 4

Gather for a meal one evening. Have each person, couple, or family bring a take-out menu from their favorite restaurant. Have each person choose what he or she might typically eat for a meal from the take-out menu. Have each person, couple, or family total up the cost of their take-out choices and put that much money in a bowl in the middle of the table. After your meeting, donate that money toward a Christian organization that feeds hungry people.

For your dinner, enjoy a simple meal that's similar to what people in many Third World countries might eat. For each person, boil ¼ cup of rice. Serve the plain boiled rice with this vegetable mixture. For every ten people, chop 1 head of cabbage and 1 onion, and dice 4 carrots. Braise or boil the veggies in chicken broth, seasoning to taste with salt and pepper. Serve water without ice during the meal.

As you eat, talk about the differences between how you eat every day with how people in poor countries eat. Some people might enjoy researching this topic. Discuss how you might change your habits to be able to contribute more to the needs of others.

Option 5

Gather for an evening of prayer. Ask God to guide your group in choosing people or an organization that you can contribute your money or other resources to. God may guide you to a needy person in your congregation, neighborhood, or community.

God may guide you to an organization that's involved with evangelism or famine relief, or to a mission church or organization. Also ask God to guide your group in deciding how much money and what other kinds of resources you can contribute. Be open and obedient to whatever God asks of you, whether God asks you to give your time, your money, or resources such as an extra car or appliance. At the end of the prayer time, collect the money or make plans to collect the resources and give them away immediately.

Debrief It

After experiencing this session's Live It activity, discuss these questions as a group:

- **On a scale of 1 (low) to 10 (high), how would you rank this experience for yourself? Why?**

- **What was the most important insight you gained from this experience?**

- **How did our activity affect the way you think about your own spiritual gifts?**

- **How might this activity change your involvement in ministry?**

- **Who in this group may have the gift of contributing to the needs of others? Explain.**

Journal It

The following space is provided for you to record
your personal thoughts, reflections, impressions, or
feelings about this session's topic and Live It activity.

Leadership

Leadership is a hot topic these days. No matter whether you're talking about it in the context of the church or in the context of corporate leadership, there is a glut of material available that promises to make you a better leader.

Our society today recognizes the advantages of having good leadership. Corporations often spend obscene amounts of money to secure people with the caliber of leadership they believe will help them find success in the marketplace. Though there is much to be learned from the examples of successful corporate leaders, their strategies and know-how will always fall short of the biblical ideal for good leaders.

The Bible recognizes the need for good, strong leadership too. However, the Bible's standards for leaders are a lot different from the corporate world's. The Bible emphasizes integrity, self-sacrifice, love, and servant-heartedness. And as our primary example, we have Jesus Christ, our Lord and commander, who laid down his life for us on the cross.

As you've discovered so far in this study, God has given his followers special gifts that we're to use to help build up and strengthen the entire body of Christ. In this session, you're going to explore the spiritual gift of leadership, discover how the gift of leadership builds up the church, and consider whether God has given you this gift.

Part 1: *learn it*

Start It *(15 minutes)*

Follow the Leader

Take turns being the leader. As the leader, you have unmitigated power to lead however you would like, but there's a catch. Your "reign" only lasts for thirty seconds. Take a moment to think about what you'd like to do when it's your turn to lead. You may want to lead the group in

- reciting the Lord's prayer,
- singing a song,
- repeating a verse you've memorized, or
- repeating an action you do.

After everyone has had an opportunity to lead, discuss these questions:

- **What was the most important element of being a successful leader in this activity?**

- **Which was more difficult, to lead or follow? Why?**

- **Were you comfortable or uncomfortable leading others? Why?**

Study It *(45-60 minutes)*

If you have a large group, form smaller groups of four to seven people to answer the discussion questions. At the end of the Study It section, allow time for the subgroups to report to the whole group.

Read Romans 12:3-8.

1. How would you describe and define the gift of leadership?

2. What does it mean to "govern diligently"? What makes a good leader?

Read Hebrews 13:7.

3. What role does the gift of leadership play in the body of Christ? Other than pastors, who else in the church leads?

4. Practically, what should leaders do? What should leaders not do?

5. Form three groups. Divide the following passages among the three groups. Read your verses and discuss how leadership is exhibited. After a few minutes, summarize your passage and share your insights with the other groups.

• Judges 4:1-9
• Nehemiah 1:1-4; 2:1-5, 11-18
• Acts 15:22-35

6. Other than Jesus, what other examples of leaders in the Bible can you think of? Are all leaders in the Bible good leaders? Explain.

"The true measure of leadership is influence—nothing more, nothing less."

John Maxwell,
The 21 Irrefutable Laws of Leadership

Read John Maxwell's quote in the margin.

7. What's true about this John Maxwell quote? Would you change or add to it?

8. Form pairs or trios, and divide the following list of verses among you. Read your verses and note what they show about Jesus as a leader and what they teach about how we can be leaders. After a few minutes, summarize your verses and share your ideas with the rest of the group.

- *Matthew 4:18-20*
- *Mark 10:35-45*
- *Mark 11:15-17*

- *Luke 6:12-13*
- *John 10:11-18*
- *John 13:12-17*

Read the quote from Bill Hybels in the margin.

9. What happens when leaders don't lead?

> "But for the church ever to reach its redemptive, life-giving potential, it must be well led...Which is why Paul cried out in Romans 12:8, 'Men and women, if you've been given the gift of leadership, for God's sake, lead.' For the world's sake, lead. For the sake of lost people, lead."
>
> **Bill Hybels, "Up to the Challenge,"** LeadershipJournal.net

10. What do you think Bill Hybels means by "well led"? Describe all the ways a church could be well led.

11. Have you ever felt that you have this gift? Why or why not? What should a person with the gift of leadership do to practice and develop this gift?

Close It *(15-30 minutes)*

Review the options in the Live It section of this session, and make plans as a group to complete one of these activities prior to moving on to the next session. This is your opportunity to move from theory to practice—*carpe diem!*

Pray It

Share prayer requests, and close in prayer. Be sure to ask God to guide your efforts as you plan and carry out a Live It activity.

Plan It

What activity are we going to do?

When are we doing this?

Where will this take place?

Other: special instructions/my responsibility

Part 2: live it

Option 1

As a group, go on a walk or a hike in territory that is unfamiliar to everyone in the group. Take turns having each member lead the hike, letting that person make any decisions that need to be made while leading. At a rest stop or at your destination, discuss the following questions:

• What was it like to lead the group into unfamiliar territory?

• If you had to make a decision about something, what was that like and how did that affect the rest of the group?

• What was it like for you when you were not at the head of the pack?

Option 2

Have each member in the group write a short devotion along with two discussion questions based on any topic or Scripture he or she wishes. Plan for an evening when everyone will take turns presenting his or her devotion, leading the discussion, and leading a closing prayer. Plan for each devotion to last five to ten minutes. At the end of the evening, discuss what it was like to lead a devotion. Did it feel natural or unnatural? Is it something you'd like to do again?

Option 3

Part of being a leader is being a vision-caster and persuading others to catch the vision. Have each group member think and pray about the direction your church, your small group, or their family should go. Then have each member present his or her "vision" to the rest of the group. After each person has had an opportunity to be a vision-caster, talk about whether the role feels comfortable or not. Did someone present a vision that you all feel particularly passionate about? Encourage anyone in your group who you feel has the gift of leadership.

Option 4

Leadership is a gift that has many applications. Have each person consider what his or her interests and talents are. For example, one person may be an expert gardener while another is a talented flutist. Have each person prayerfully come up with a strategic plan for how someone could help build up the church by leading in his or her specific area of expertise. Be as detail-oriented and as practical as possible. Then have each person present his or her plan to the rest of the group. Does anyone feel particularly passionate about his or her plan? Encourage each other to put your plans in action if you feel God leading you in that direction.

Option 5

Plan to gather for a frank discussion about leadership in your group. Consider these questions:

• Who in our group tends to be a leader?

• Do different people in our group tend to lead different kinds of activities?

• Do people in our group lead in other contexts or situations?

• What specifically are we skilled at leading? Are there areas where we could use more skilled leadership?

• Are there people in our group who prefer *not* to lead anything? (Remember: Not everyone can be a leader. There needs to be skilled followers, too!) What are their gifts?

• Is our group advantageously using its leadership skills? What do we do well?

• Is there something we should be doing differently or more of?

You may find that there are a number of leaders in your group who aren't effectively using their gift of leadership for the building of God's kingdom. Encourage each other to fully use your gifts to the glory of God.

Debrief It

After experiencing this session's Live It activity, discuss these questions as a group:

- **On a scale of 1 (low) to 10 (high), how would you rank this experience for yourself? Why?**

- **What was the most important insight you gained from this experience?**

- **How did our activity affect the way you think about your own spiritual gifts?**

- **How might this activity change your involvement in ministry?**

- **Who in this group may have the gift of leadership? Explain.**

The following space is provided for you to record your personal thoughts, reflections, impressions, or feelings about this session's topic and Live It activity.

Mercy

Mercy, or compassion, is a core identity of the followers of Christ because our mercy is an earthly expression of the very nature of our loving God. Micah 6:8 tells us that we are to live balanced lives of acting justly and loving mercy. And Jesus tells us, "Blessed are the merciful" (Matthew 5:7). According to the Gospels, Jesus was moved to compassion by both the physical and emotional needs of the people around him. Clearly, living like Christ requires that we be open and caring about those in all kinds of need.

Some people, however, are gifted in mercy. They are the people in our midst who find their spiritual fulfillment in compassionately meeting the needs of people around them. It is not only the great needs that move them to action. They have the ability to see the little opportunities for showing tangible evidence of the love of God. Mercy can be lived out as a quiet, behind-the-scenes kind of gift. Combined with the gifts of preaching or exhorting, the gift of mercy can fuel sweeping social movements.

This lesson will give you the opportunity to examine some lives motivated by the gift of mercy and to better understand how this gift can enrich the functioning of the entire church.

Start It *(15 minutes)*

Mercy Me!

> **Leader:** Before the group meets, put one bandage, one paper clip, one coin, and one greeting card in a lunch-size paper bag for every four people.

Form groups of four. Take the bag your leader gives you and have each person reach in the bag and pull out one item. Note what your item represents.

Bandage—a time someone helped you during physical illness or injury.

Paper clip—a time someone saw your helplessness and helped you "get it together."

Coin—a time someone helped you with a financial or material need.

Greeting card—a time someone saw your distress and showed you special kindness.

Share with your group of four a story from your life prompted by the item you pulled from the bag. When everyone has shared a story, join the rest of the group, and discuss these questions:

- **How do these stories from our lives show what it means to be merciful?**

- **How did the act of mercy you experienced impact you at the time?**

- **Was the act done for you characteristic of the individual who showed mercy to you? In what way?**

Study It *(45-60 minutes)*

> If you have a large group, form smaller groups of four to seven people to answer the discussion questions. At the end of the Study It section, allow time for the subgroups to report to the whole group.

Read Romans 12:3-8 and the margin note.

1. What is mercy? What role does the spiritual gift of mercy play in the body of Christ? What role might mercy play in ministry outside the church?

> The *Amplified Bible* expands our understanding of mercy with this rendering of Luke 6:36: "So be merciful (sympathetic, tender, responsive and compassionate)."

2. What's the significance of the instruction to show mercy cheerfully?

3. Who do you know who is merciful? What does this person do that indicates he or she is merciful?

The gift of mercy has often been seen in people who started or expanded great social movements. William Booth, who, along with his wife, Catherine, founded the Salvation Army, is one such example.

"While women weep as they do now, I'll fight; while little children go hungry as they do now, I'll fight; while men go to prison, in and out, in and out, as they do now, I'll fight; while there is a drunkard left, while there is a poor lost girl on the streets, while there remains one dark soul without the light of God, I'll fight—I'll fight to the very end."

William Booth, in his last public address

Read the margin note about William Booth.

4. How does this quotation affect the way you understand mercy? What does a merciful person think, feel, and do?

5. Form pairs or trios, and divide the following list of verses among you. Read your verses and note what you learn about mercy. After a few minutes, summarize your verses and share your ideas with the rest of the group.

- *Hosea 6:6*
- *Micah 6:8*
- *Zechariah 7:8-10*
- *Matthew 5:7*

- *Matthew 23:23-24*
- *Luke 6:35-36*
- *James 3:17*
- *Jude 22-23*

Read Luke 10:25-37.

6. How does this story epitomize mercy?

Read Matthew 9:9-13.

7. How did Jesus express mercy? How is that similar to or different from the ways we show mercy?

Read the quotation from the early-church father St. John Chrysostom.

8. How might mercy disappoint Satan? How is mercy an important tool in our work to build God's kingdom?

"Mercy imitates God and disappoints Satan."

St. John Chrysostom

Read Matthew 18:23-33 and Matthew 25:34-40.

9. Why should we practice mercy? What keeps us from being merciful? What can we do to set aside those hindrances?

10. Have you ever felt that you have the gift of mercy? Why or why not? What should a person with the gift of mercy do to practice and develop this gift?

Close It *(15-30 minutes)*

Review the options in the Live It section of this session, and make plans as a group to complete one of these activities prior to moving on to the next session. This is your opportunity to move from theory to practice—*carpe diem!*

Pray It

Share prayer requests, and close in prayer. Be sure to ask God to guide your efforts as you plan and carry out a Live It activity.

Since this is the last session in this study, discuss what the group would like to do next. You may want to have a party to celebrate the completion of this course.

Plan It

What activity are we going to do?

When are we doing this?

Where will this take place?

Other: special instructions/my responsibility

Prayer Requests

Option 1

Get involved in your county's foster-care system. Learn as much as you can about the children typically served in your area. Call your county's child services department and find out how you can help. Some areas welcome having small stuffed animals, blankets, picture books, toiletries, formula, or diapers given to be used by children when they come under the protection of the department. Gather supplies, and donate them to the department. Some in your group may be moved to sign up to be foster parents.

Option 2

Volunteer to help in your community's alternative high school. Such schools often serve at-risk teenagers or teenagers who've been in trouble with the law or have substance-abuse problems. Some teenagers are responsible for providing a living for themselves. Others must juggle the responsibilities of school and children. Still others struggle to learn despite having learning disabilities. Perhaps the school in your community could use mentors. Perhaps your group could teach special skills in the school. Perhaps the group could take a turn caring for the students' children.

Option 3

Volunteer one evening to visit patients at your local hospice. Offer to sit with the patients, read to them, pray with them, or just listen. Bring small, cheery gifts such as flowers, or combine forces with a children's Sunday school class in your church and have the children make get-well cards for the patients. If there are musicians in your group, find out if the facility would welcome a concert.

Option 4

There are many countries in which orphaned children have little hope for a good life. In some countries, orphans live in garbage dumps and make their living by going through the garbage. In other countries, disabled children are forgotten in sterile hospitals with substandard care and no one to show them love. Find out what your church or denomination is doing to help orphans in other countries, and see how your group can get involved. Another way to help is to get involved with organizations such as World Vision and Compassion International.

Option 5

Merciful people often take up the cause for those who are too weak or powerless to protect themselves. Investigate in your area and find a group of people who need help. Perhaps there are many homeless people in your area. Or perhaps there are many children with parents in prison. Or perhaps there are many elderly in your area who are separated from their families. Discuss what your group can do financially, socially, and politically to show mercy to that group. Then carry out your plans.

Bonus Option

Now that you've completed this course on spiritual gifts and have a better idea of what the Bible says about spiritual gifts, have each group member take a spiritual gifts inventory assessment. Talk about how this course, plus the inventory, plus your own reflection and prayer time has affected what you think about the gifts God has given you. Talk about how you plan to put your gifts into practice for the building of God's kingdom.

Debrief It

After experiencing this session's Live It activity, discuss these questions as a group:

- **On a scale of 1 (low) to 10 (high), how would you rank this experience for yourself? Why?**

- **What was the most important insight you gained from this experience?**

- **How did our activity affect the way you think about your own spiritual gifts?**

- **How might this activity change your involvement in ministry?**

- **Who in this group may have the gift of mercy? Explain.**

The following space is provided for you to record your personal thoughts, reflections, impressions, or feelings about this session's topic and Live It activity.